Cloth & Comfort
Stitch-Crafting Journal

Roderick Kiracofe

POTTER STYLE

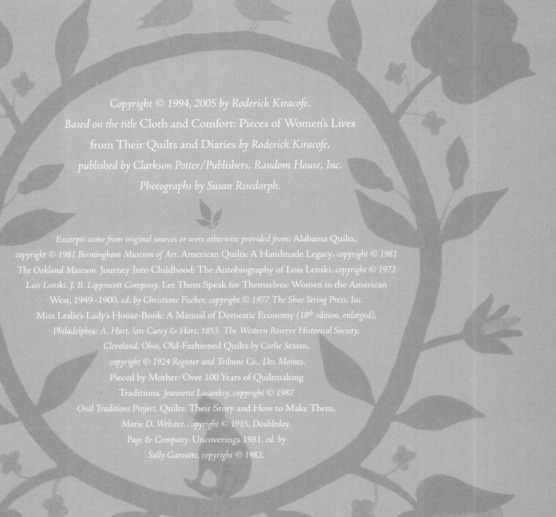

Introduction

Sewing and needlework projects, like diaries, are an accumulation of bits and pieces of the maker's life, a repository of ideas, hopes, and feelings. If you are drawn to working with fabric, you undoubtedly feel a connection to the history of your craft and are aware of the little story that you create by bringing together different materials. This journal is the perfect place for keeping a diary of your handmade treasures, with pages designed for attaching fabric swatches, sketching ideas, and pasting in photos. It's a workbook and memory book all in one, because there are so many practical and sentimental reasons for making a record of your handwork.

The history of stitch-crafting is filled with the dual spirit of practicality and senti- mentality. Making clothes and quilts was frequently a matter of necessity, but by making them beautiful, women turned their work into an outlet for creativity and self- expression. This journal is sprinkled with voices from the past— from bits and pieces of stories, letters, inscriptions, household ledgers, and diary entries written by women whose memories remain intact in both their words and their stitch-work. These writings form a picture of women in the late-nineteenth and early-twentieth centuries sewing and filling up the minutes and hours of their days either as a part of their chores or after the "work" was done.

Inevitably, references to these hours of labor filled their records of daily life—"This is the last day of October and what a big days work I have done I comenced [*sic*] to sew at day light this morning and it is <u>most</u> sundown." These written remem- brances, largely private thoughts and often anonymous, were rarely meant for anyone else to read. They are leftover pieces, patches of time that will never come again, threaded together with needlework memorabilia and details of quilts about which women wrote—and for which they felt justifiable, quiet pride.

Life on the American frontier could be hard and lonely, but sewing and quilt making often provided warmth in more than the obvious ways. "For the winter I think I shall make a quilt to keep from getting lonesome," a woman from Minnesota wrote to a friend. To survive the solitude, friends and relatives in distant locales sometimes enclosed in their letters swatches of cloth from quilts or dresses they were making as a tactile reminder of themselves. These bits of shared material were often saved as a keepsake or incorporated into a quilt. In such ways, cloth came to be indelibly imprinted with comforting references, and the quilts made from these pieces became potent reminders of loved ones.

While sewing, particularly quilting, was sometimes a social event, more often it was a solitary, repetitive activity, a necessary task in order to clothe one's family at a time when store-bought goods were still a luxury. "I am weary," Ruth Anna Abrams, an Indiana housewife, confesses to her diary in 1881. "I have sewed hard all day." She had reason to feel tired. Abrams bore a total of nine children, the last delivered at home late in the year she was writing, with only her husband at hand to help—"a hard man to keep in good humor," she wrote of him privately. How she found time to keep a journal at all is a wonder. And yet she found it in herself, like many of these women, to collect her thoughts and mark the passage of time with a diary.

These written fragments from the past are a wonderful reminder that each individual life is itself a patchwork of experiences, both dramatic and mundane. Surprisingly, it is often the mundane rather than the dramatic that speaks to us across the years, linking the past to our own lives. Your stitching projects contain a history of your daily life: the time you spend on a project, the story behind the materials you use, and the experience that inspires your design. Even if you use this journal for the most practical aspects of crafting, the end result will still be a record of the time, thought, and creativity that went into each piece.

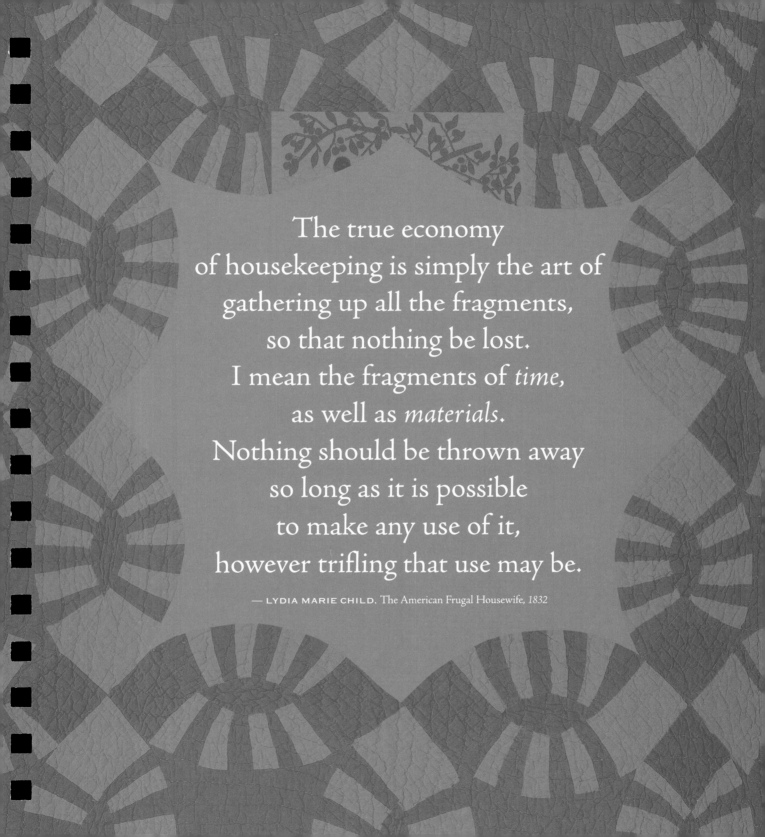

The true economy
of housekeeping is simply the art of
gathering up all the fragments,
so that nothing be lost.
I mean the fragments of *time*,
as well as *materials*.
Nothing should be thrown away
so long as it is possible
to make any use of it,
however trifling that use may be.

— LYDIA MARIE CHILD, The American Frugal Housewife, *1832*

14. Friday

get up very early
ache worked
st all day In the
wn town and broug
cloth, costing in all
nd a little in the
letter to H F M

PROJECT

DATE STARTED

DATE COMPLETED

REASON FOR STARTING THE PROJECT

MATERIALS USED

SOURCES OF MATERIALS

MY INSPIRATION FOR THIS PROJECT

DIMENSIONS

FABRIC SWATCHES AND THREAD SAMPLES

PHOTO OF FINISHED PROJECT

PROJECT

DATE STARTED

DATE COMPLETED

REASON FOR STARTING THE PROJECT

MATERIALS USED

SOURCES OF MATERIALS

MY INSPIRATION FOR THIS PROJECT

DIMENSIONS

FABRIC SWATCHES AND THREAD SAMPLES

PHOTO OF FINISHED PROJECT

PROJECT

DATE STARTED

DATE COMPLETED

REASON FOR STARTING THE PROJECT

MATERIALS USED

SOURCES OF MATERIALS

MY INSPIRATION FOR THIS PROJECT

DIMENSIONS

FABRIC SWATCHES AND THREAD SAMPLES

PHOTO OF FINISHED PROJECT

PROJECT

DATE STARTED

....

DATE COMPLETED

REASON FOR STARTING THE PROJECT

....

....

....

....

MATERIALS USED

....

....

....

....

SOURCES OF MATERIALS

....

....

....

....

MY INSPIRATION FOR THIS PROJECT

....

....

....

....

DIMENSIONS

FABRIC SWATCHES AND THREAD SAMPLES

PHOTO OF FINISHED PROJECT

PROJECT

DATE STARTED

PHOTO OF FINISHED PROJECT

DATE COMPLETED

REASON FOR STARTING THE PROJECT

MATERIALS USED

SOURCES OF MATERIALS

MY INSPIRATION FOR THIS PROJECT

DIMENSIONS

FABRIC SWATCHES AND THREAD SAMPLES

E very young girl should piece one quilt at least to carry away with her to husband's home, and if her lot happens to be cast among strangers, as is often the case, the quilt when she unfolds it will seem like the face of a familiar friend.

— Good Housekeeping, *April 14, 1888*

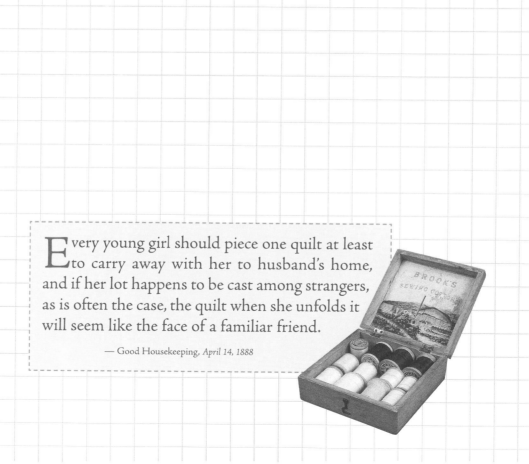

PROJECT

DATE STARTED

DATE COMPLETED

REASON FOR STARTING THE PROJECT

MATERIALS USED

SOURCES OF MATERIALS

MY INSPIRATION FOR THIS PROJECT

DIMENSIONS

FABRIC SWATCHES AND THREAD SAMPLES

PHOTO OF FINISHED PROJECT

PROJECT

DATE STARTED

DATE COMPLETED

REASON FOR STARTING THE PROJECT

MATERIALS USED

SOURCES OF MATERIALS

MY INSPIRATION FOR THIS PROJECT

DIMENSIONS

FABRIC SWATCHES AND THREAD SAMPLES

PHOTO OF FINISHED PROJECT

PROJECT

DATE STARTED

DATE COMPLETED

REASON FOR STARTING THE PROJECT

MATERIALS USED

SOURCES OF MATERIALS

MY INSPIRATION FOR THIS PROJECT

DIMENSIONS

FABRIC SWATCHES AND THREAD SAMPLES

PHOTO OF FINISHED PROJECT

PROJECT

DATE STARTED

PHOTO OF FINISHED PROJECT

DATE COMPLETED

REASON FOR STARTING THE PROJECT

MATERIALS USED

SOURCES OF MATERIALS

MY INSPIRATION FOR THIS PROJECT

DIMENSIONS

FABRIC SWATCHES AND THREAD SAMPLES

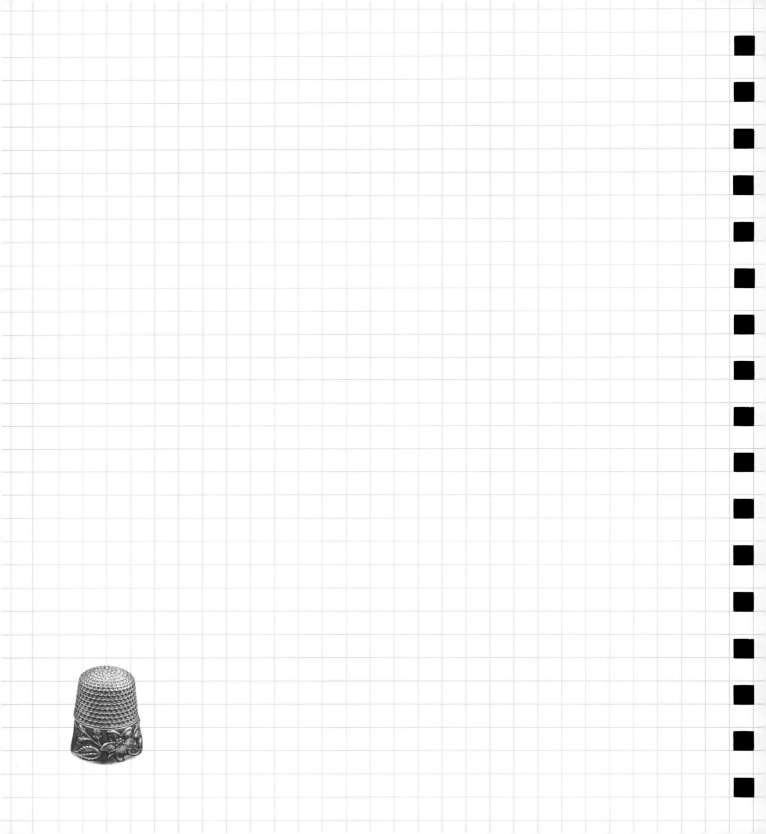

PROJECT

DATE STARTED

DATE COMPLETED

REASON FOR STARTING THE PROJECT

MATERIALS USED

SOURCES OF MATERIALS

MY INSPIRATION FOR THIS PROJECT

DIMENSIONS

FABRIC SWATCHES AND THREAD SAMPLES

PHOTO OF FINISHED PROJECT

PROJECT

DATE STARTED

DATE COMPLETED

REASON FOR STARTING THE PROJECT

MATERIALS USED

SOURCES OF MATERIALS

MY INSPIRATION FOR THIS PROJECT

DIMENSIONS

FABRIC SWATCHES AND THREAD SAMPLES

PHOTO OF FINISHED PROJECT

PROJECT

DATE STARTED

DATE COMPLETED

REASON FOR STARTING THE PROJECT

MATERIALS USED

SOURCES OF MATERIALS

MY INSPIRATION FOR THIS PROJECT

DIMENSIONS

FABRIC SWATCHES AND THREAD SAMPLES

PHOTO OF FINISHED PROJECT

To make a silk quilt—This
is a light and convenient article
for a couch or for a child's crib,
and will be found extremely
useful in the sick-room. It can
be made very economically out
of two silk dresses, after the
bodies are past wear.

— *From* Miss Leslie's Lady's House-Book:
A Manual of Domestic Economy

PROJECT

DATE STARTED

PHOTO OF FINISHED PROJECT

DATE COMPLETED

REASON FOR STARTING THE PROJECT

MATERIALS USED

SOURCES OF MATERIALS

MY INSPIRATION FOR THIS PROJECT

DIMENSIONS

FABRIC SWATCHES AND THREAD SAMPLES

PROJECT

DATE STARTED

DATE COMPLETED

REASON FOR STARTING THE PROJECT

MATERIALS USED

SOURCES OF MATERIALS

MY INSPIRATION FOR THIS PROJECT

DIMENSIONS

FABRIC SWATCHES AND THREAD SAMPLES

PHOTO OF FINISHED PROJECT

PROJECT

DATE STARTED

PHOTO OF FINISHED PROJECT

DATE COMPLETED

REASON FOR STARTING THE PROJECT

MATERIALS USED

SOURCES OF MATERIALS

MY INSPIRATION FOR THIS PROJECT

DIMENSIONS

FABRIC SWATCHES AND THREAD SAMPLES

PROJECT

DATE STARTED

....

DATE COMPLETED

REASON FOR STARTING THE PROJECT

MATERIALS USED

SOURCES OF MATERIALS

MY INSPIRATION FOR THIS PROJECT

DIMENSIONS

FABRIC SWATCHES AND THREAD SAMPLES

PHOTO OF FINISHED PROJECT

PROJECT

DATE STARTED

DATE COMPLETED

REASON FOR STARTING THE PROJECT

MATERIALS USED

SOURCES OF MATERIALS

MY INSPIRATION FOR THIS PROJECT

DIMENSIONS

FABRIC SWATCHES AND THREAD SAMPLES

PHOTO OF FINISHED PROJECT

PROJECT

DATE STARTED
....

DATE COMPLETED

REASON FOR STARTING THE PROJECT
....
....
....
....

MATERIALS USED
....
....
....
....

SOURCES OF MATERIALS
....
....
....
....

MY INSPIRATION FOR THIS PROJECT
....
....
....
....

DIMENSIONS

FABRIC SWATCHES AND THREAD SAMPLES

PHOTO OF FINISHED PROJECT

PROJECT

PHOTO OF FINISHED PROJECT

DATE STARTED

DATE COMPLETED

REASON FOR STARTING THE PROJECT

MATERIALS USED

SOURCES OF MATERIALS

MY INSPIRATION FOR THIS PROJECT

DIMENSIONS

FABRIC SWATCHES AND THREAD SAMPLES

I was permitted
to have material
with which I cut
out, fitted, and
made on the sewing
machine a dress
for my sister when
I was eleven.
Of this I was
justly proud.

— EDITH WHITE,
from her 1936 memoir

PROJECT

DATE STARTED

DATE COMPLETED

REASON FOR STARTING THE PROJECT

MATERIALS USED

SOURCES OF MATERIALS

MY INSPIRATION FOR THIS PROJECT

DIMENSIONS

FABRIC SWATCHES AND THREAD SAMPLES

PHOTO OF FINISHED PROJECT

PROJECT

DATE STARTED

DATE COMPLETED

REASON FOR STARTING THE PROJECT

MATERIALS USED

SOURCES OF MATERIALS

MY INSPIRATION FOR THIS PROJECT

DIMENSIONS

FABRIC SWATCHES AND THREAD SAMPLES

PHOTO OF FINISHED PROJECT

PROJECT

DATE STARTED

DATE COMPLETED

REASON FOR STARTING THE PROJECT

MATERIALS USED

SOURCES OF MATERIALS

MY INSPIRATION FOR THIS PROJECT

DIMENSIONS

FABRIC SWATCHES AND THREAD SAMPLES

PHOTO OF FINISHED PROJECT

PROJECT

DATE STARTED

PHOTO OF FINISHED PROJECT

DATE COMPLETED

REASON FOR STARTING THE PROJECT

MATERIALS USED

SOURCES OF MATERIALS

MY INSPIRATION FOR THIS PROJECT

DIMENSIONS

FABRIC SWATCHES AND THREAD SAMPLES

PROJECT

DATE STARTED

DATE COMPLETED

REASON FOR STARTING THE PROJECT

MATERIALS USED

SOURCES OF MATERIALS

MY INSPIRATION FOR THIS PROJECT

DIMENSIONS

FABRIC SWATCHES AND THREAD SAMPLES

PHOTO OF FINISHED PROJECT

PROJECT

DATE STARTED

DATE COMPLETED

REASON FOR STARTING THE PROJECT

MATERIALS USED

SOURCES OF MATERIALS

MY INSPIRATION FOR THIS PROJECT

DIMENSIONS

FABRIC SWATCHES AND THREAD SAMPLES

PHOTO OF FINISHED PROJECT

PROJECT

DATE STARTED

DATE COMPLETED

REASON FOR STARTING THE PROJECT

MATERIALS USED

SOURCES OF MATERIALS

MY INSPIRATION FOR THIS PROJECT

DIMENSIONS

FABRIC SWATCHES AND THREAD SAMPLES

PHOTO OF FINISHED PROJECT

As lonely through this world I stray,
And pass the pensive hours;
May truth and virtue point the way
And strewn my path with flowers.
M.E. Peach, Maryland 1850

— *Quilt inscription*

PROJECT

DATE STARTED

....

DATE COMPLETED

REASON FOR STARTING THE PROJECT

....

....

....

....

MATERIALS USED

....

....

....

....

SOURCES OF MATERIALS

....

....

....

....

MY INSPIRATION FOR THIS PROJECT

....

....

....

....

DIMENSIONS

FABRIC SWATCHES AND THREAD SAMPLES

PHOTO OF FINISHED PROJECT

PROJECT

DATE STARTED

PHOTO OF FINISHED PROJECT

DATE COMPLETED

REASON FOR STARTING THE PROJECT

MATERIALS USED

SOURCES OF MATERIALS

MY INSPIRATION FOR THIS PROJECT

DIMENSIONS

FABRIC SWATCHES AND THREAD SAMPLES

PROJECT

DATE STARTED

DATE COMPLETED

REASON FOR STARTING THE PROJECT

MATERIALS USED

SOURCES OF MATERIALS

MY INSPIRATION FOR THIS PROJECT

DIMENSIONS

FABRIC SWATCHES AND THREAD SAMPLES

PHOTO OF FINISHED PROJECT

PROJECT

DATE STARTED

DATE COMPLETED

REASON FOR STARTING THE PROJECT

MATERIALS USED

SOURCES OF MATERIALS

MY INSPIRATION FOR THIS PROJECT

DIMENSIONS

FABRIC SWATCHES AND THREAD SAMPLES

PHOTO OF FINISHED PROJECT

PROJECT

DATE STARTED

PHOTO OF FINISHED PROJECT

DATE COMPLETED

REASON FOR STARTING THE PROJECT

MATERIALS USED

SOURCES OF MATERIALS

MY INSPIRATION FOR THIS PROJECT

DIMENSIONS

FABRIC SWATCHES AND THREAD SAMPLES

PROJECT

DATE STARTED

PHOTO OF FINISHED PROJECT

DATE COMPLETED

REASON FOR STARTING THE PROJECT

MATERIALS USED

SOURCES OF MATERIALS

MY INSPIRATION FOR THIS PROJECT

DIMENSIONS

FABRIC SWATCHES AND THREAD SAMPLES

PROJECT

DATE STARTED

DATE COMPLETED

REASON FOR STARTING THE PROJECT

MATERIALS USED

SOURCES OF MATERIALS

MY INSPIRATION FOR THIS PROJECT

DIMENSIONS

FABRIC SWATCHES AND THREAD SAMPLES

PHOTO OF FINISHED PROJECT

PROJECT

DATE STARTED

DATE COMPLETED

REASON FOR STARTING THE PROJECT

MATERIALS USED

SOURCES OF MATERIALS

MY INSPIRATION FOR THIS PROJECT

DIMENSIONS

FABRIC SWATCHES AND THREAD SAMPLES

PHOTO OF FINISHED PROJECT

The number of quilts which are never used, but which are most carefully treasured by their owners on account of some sentimental or historic association, is far greater than generally supposed.

— *From Marie D. Webster's 1915 book*, Quilts: Their Story and How to Make Them

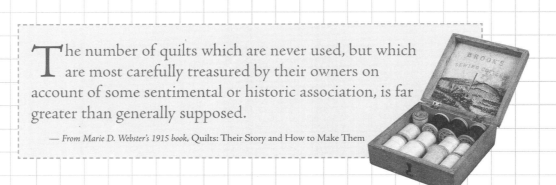

PROJECT

DATE STARTED

DATE COMPLETED

REASON FOR STARTING THE PROJECT

MATERIALS USED

SOURCES OF MATERIALS

MY INSPIRATION FOR THIS PROJECT

DIMENSIONS

FABRIC SWATCHES AND THREAD SAMPLES

PHOTO OF FINISHED PROJECT

PROJECT

DATE STARTED

....

DATE COMPLETED

REASON FOR STARTING THE PROJECT

....
....
....
....

MATERIALS USED

....
....
....
....

SOURCES OF MATERIALS

....
....
....
....

MY INSPIRATION FOR THIS PROJECT

....
....
....
....

DIMENSIONS

FABRIC SWATCHES AND THREAD SAMPLES

PHOTO OF FINISHED PROJECT

PROJECT

DATE STARTED

DATE COMPLETED

REASON FOR STARTING THE PROJECT

MATERIALS USED

SOURCES OF MATERIALS

MY INSPIRATION FOR THIS PROJECT

DIMENSIONS

FABRIC SWATCHES AND THREAD SAMPLES

PHOTO OF FINISHED PROJECT

PROJECT

DATE STARTED

PHOTO OF FINISHED PROJECT

DATE COMPLETED

REASON FOR STARTING THE PROJECT

MATERIALS USED

SOURCES OF MATERIALS

MY INSPIRATION FOR THIS PROJECT

DIMENSIONS

FABRIC SWATCHES AND THREAD SAMPLES

PROJECT

DATE STARTED

DATE COMPLETED

REASON FOR STARTING THE PROJECT

MATERIALS USED

SOURCES OF MATERIALS

MY INSPIRATION FOR THIS PROJECT

DIMENSIONS

FABRIC SWATCHES AND THREAD SAMPLES

PHOTO OF FINISHED PROJECT

PROJECT

DATE STARTED
....

DATE COMPLETED
_____

REASON FOR STARTING THE PROJECT
....
....
....
....
_____

MATERIALS USED
....
....
....
....
_____

SOURCES OF MATERIALS
....
....
....
....
_____

MY INSPIRATION FOR THIS PROJECT
....
....
....
....
_____

DIMENSIONS
_____

FABRIC SWATCHES AND THREAD SAMPLES

PHOTO OF FINISHED PROJECT

PROJECT

PHOTO OF FINISHED PROJECT

DATE STARTED

DATE COMPLETED

REASON FOR STARTING THE PROJECT

MATERIALS USED

SOURCES OF MATERIALS

MY INSPIRATION FOR THIS PROJECT

DIMENSIONS

FABRIC SWATCHES AND THREAD SAMPLES

PROJECT

DATE STARTED

DATE COMPLETED

REASON FOR STARTING THE PROJECT

MATERIALS USED

SOURCES OF MATERIALS

MY INSPIRATION FOR THIS PROJECT

DIMENSIONS

FABRIC SWATCHES AND THREAD SAMPLES

PHOTO OF FINISHED PROJECT

After 47 years of assiduous labor, Mrs. S. Lizzie Weaves, a Bridgeton, N.J. woman, has just finished a crazy quilt of 30,075 patches.

— Kent News, *Chestertown, Maryland, January 4, 1890*

PROJECT

DATE STARTED

PHOTO OF FINISHED PROJECT

DATE COMPLETED

REASON FOR STARTING THE PROJECT

MATERIALS USED

SOURCES OF MATERIALS

MY INSPIRATION FOR THIS PROJECT

DIMENSIONS

FABRIC SWATCHES AND THREAD SAMPLES

PROJECT

DATE STARTED

PHOTO OF FINISHED PROJECT

DATE COMPLETED

REASON FOR STARTING THE PROJECT

MATERIALS USED

SOURCES OF MATERIALS

MY INSPIRATION FOR THIS PROJECT

DIMENSIONS

FABRIC SWATCHES AND THREAD SAMPLES

PROJECT

DATE STARTED

DATE COMPLETED

REASON FOR STARTING THE PROJECT

MATERIALS USED

SOURCES OF MATERIALS

MY INSPIRATION FOR THIS PROJECT

DIMENSIONS

FABRIC SWATCHES AND THREAD SAMPLES

PHOTO OF FINISHED PROJECT

PROJECT

DATE STARTED

DATE COMPLETED

REASON FOR STARTING THE PROJECT

MATERIALS USED

SOURCES OF MATERIALS

MY INSPIRATION FOR THIS PROJECT

DIMENSIONS

FABRIC SWATCHES AND THREAD SAMPLES

PHOTO OF FINISHED PROJECT

PROJECT

DATE STARTED

DATE COMPLETED

REASON FOR STARTING THE PROJECT

MATERIALS USED

SOURCES OF MATERIALS

MY INSPIRATION FOR THIS PROJECT

DIMENSIONS

FABRIC SWATCHES AND THREAD SAMPLES

PHOTO OF FINISHED PROJECT

PROJECT

DATE STARTED

....

DATE COMPLETED

_____

REASON FOR STARTING THE PROJECT

....

....

....

....

_____

MATERIALS USED

....

....

....

....

_____

SOURCES OF MATERIALS

....

....

....

....

_____

MY INSPIRATION FOR THIS PROJECT

....

....

....

....

_____

DIMENSIONS

_____

FABRIC SWATCHES AND THREAD SAMPLES

PHOTO OF FINISHED PROJECT

PROJECT

DATE STARTED

DATE COMPLETED

REASON FOR STARTING THE PROJECT

MATERIALS USED

SOURCES OF MATERIALS

MY INSPIRATION FOR THIS PROJECT

DIMENSIONS

FABRIC SWATCHES AND THREAD SAMPLES

PHOTO OF FINISHED PROJECT

Dear old-fashioned quilts with your patches so gay,
You retain all the charm of an earlier day;
Like the old-fashioned garden our grandmothers grew,
Our love never wanes for them or you.
Carlie Sexton

—*Quilt inscription*

PROJECT

DATE STARTED

DATE COMPLETED

REASON FOR STARTING THE PROJECT

MATERIALS USED

SOURCES OF MATERIALS

MY INSPIRATION FOR THIS PROJECT

DIMENSIONS

FABRIC SWATCHES AND THREAD SAMPLES

PHOTO OF FINISHED PROJECT

PROJECT

DATE STARTED
....

DATE COMPLETED
_____

REASON FOR STARTING THE PROJECT
....
....
....
....
_____

MATERIALS USED
....
....
....
....
_____

SOURCES OF MATERIALS
....
....
....
....
_____

MY INSPIRATION FOR THIS PROJECT
....
....
....
....
_____

DIMENSIONS
_____

FABRIC SWATCHES AND THREAD SAMPLES

PHOTO OF FINISHED PROJECT

PROJECT

PHOTO OF FINISHED PROJECT

DATE STARTED

DATE COMPLETED

REASON FOR STARTING THE PROJECT

MATERIALS USED

SOURCES OF MATERIALS

MY INSPIRATION FOR THIS PROJECT

DIMENSIONS

FABRIC SWATCHES AND THREAD SAMPLES

PROJECT

DATE STARTED

....

DATE COMPLETED

REASON FOR STARTING THE PROJECT

....

....

....

....

MATERIALS USED

....

....

....

....

SOURCES OF MATERIALS

....

....

....

....

MY INSPIRATION FOR THIS PROJECT

....

....

....

....

DIMENSIONS

FABRIC SWATCHES AND THREAD SAMPLES

PHOTO OF FINISHED PROJECT

3674
A

674
C

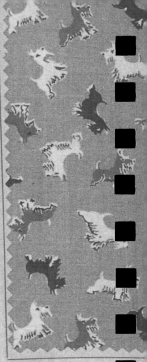

FABRIC

STORE	STORE
LOCATION	LOCATION
HOURS	HOURS
PHONE NUMBER	PHONE NUMBER
WEBSITE	WEBSITE
E-MAIL	E-MAIL

STORE	STORE
LOCATION	LOCATION
HOURS	HOURS
PHONE NUMBER	PHONE NUMBER
WEBSITE	WEBSITE
E-MAIL	E-MAIL

STORE	STORE
LOCATION	LOCATION
HOURS	HOURS
PHONE NUMBER	PHONE NUMBER
WEBSITE	WEBSITE
E-MAIL	E-MAIL

FABRIC

STORE

LOCATION

HOURS

PHONE NUMBER

WEBSITE

E-MAIL

STORE

LOCATION

HOURS

PHONE NUMBER

WEBSITE

E-MAIL

STORE

LOCATION

HOURS

PHONE NUMBER

WEBSITE

E-MAIL

STORE

LOCATION

HOURS

PHONE NUMBER

WEBSITE

E-MAIL

STORE

LOCATION

HOURS

PHONE NUMBER

WEBSITE

E-MAIL

STORE

LOCATION

HOURS

PHONE NUMBER

WEBSITE

E-MAIL

TRIMMING

STORE	STORE
LOCATION	LOCATION
HOURS	HOURS
PHONE NUMBER	PHONE NUMBER
WEBSITE	WEBSITE
E-MAIL	E-MAIL

STORE	STORE
LOCATION	LOCATION
HOURS	HOURS
PHONE NUMBER	PHONE NUMBER
WEBSITE	WEBSITE
E-MAIL	E-MAIL

STORE	STORE
LOCATION	LOCATION
HOURS	HOURS
PHONE NUMBER	PHONE NUMBER
WEBSITE	WEBSITE
E-MAIL	E-MAIL

TRIMMING

STORE	STORE
LOCATION	LOCATION
HOURS	HOURS
PHONE NUMBER	PHONE NUMBER
WEBSITE	WEBSITE
E-MAIL	E-MAIL
STORE	STORE
LOCATION	LOCATION
HOURS	HOURS
PHONE NUMBER	PHONE NUMBER
WEBSITE	WEBSITE
E-MAIL	E-MAIL
STORE	STORE
LOCATION	LOCATION
HOURS	HOURS
PHONE NUMBER	PHONE NUMBER
WEBSITE	WEBSITE
E-MAIL	E-MAIL

NOTIONS

STORE

LOCATION

HOURS

PHONE NUMBER

WEBSITE

E-MAIL

STORE

LOCATION

HOURS

PHONE NUMBER

WEBSITE

E-MAIL

STORE

LOCATION

HOURS

PHONE NUMBER

WEBSITE

E-MAIL

STORE

LOCATION

HOURS

PHONE NUMBER

WEBSITE

E-MAIL

STORE

LOCATION

HOURS

PHONE NUMBER

WEBSITE

E-MAIL

STORE

LOCATION

HOURS

PHONE NUMBER

WEBSITE

E-MAIL

NOTIONS

STORE

STORE

LOCATION

LOCATION

HOURS

HOURS

PHONE NUMBER

PHONE NUMBER

WEBSITE

WEBSITE

E-MAIL

E-MAIL

STORE

STORE

LOCATION

LOCATION

HOURS

HOURS

PHONE NUMBER

PHONE NUMBER

WEBSITE

WEBSITE

E-MAIL

E-MAIL

STORE

STORE

LOCATION

LOCATION

HOURS

HOURS

PHONE NUMBER

PHONE NUMBER

WEBSITE

WEBSITE

E-MAIL

E-MAIL

ANTIQUE/VINTAGE MATERIALS

STORE

LOCATION

HOURS

PHONE NUMBER

WEBSITE

E-MAIL

STORE

LOCATION

HOURS

PHONE NUMBER

WEBSITE

E-MAIL

STORE

LOCATION

HOURS

PHONE NUMBER

WEBSITE

E-MAIL

STORE

LOCATION

HOURS

PHONE NUMBER

WEBSITE

E-MAIL

STORE

LOCATION

HOURS

PHONE NUMBER

WEBSITE

E-MAIL

STORE

LOCATION

HOURS

PHONE NUMBER

WEBSITE

E-MAIL

ANTIQUE/VINTAGE MATERIALS

STORE

LOCATION

HOURS

PHONE NUMBER

WEBSITE

E-MAIL

STORE

LOCATION

HOURS

PHONE NUMBER

WEBSITE

E-MAIL

STORE

LOCATION

HOURS

PHONE NUMBER

WEBSITE

E-MAIL

STORE

LOCATION

HOURS

PHONE NUMBER

WEBSITE

E-MAIL

STORE

LOCATION

HOURS

PHONE NUMBER

WEBSITE

E-MAIL

STORE

LOCATION

HOURS

PHONE NUMBER

WEBSITE

E-MAIL

FLEA MARKETS

MARKET

LOCATION

TIME OF YEAR/HOURS

MARKET

LOCATION

TIME OF YEAR/HOURS

MARKET

LOCATION

TIME OF YEAR/HOURS

MARKET

LOCATION

TIME OF YEAR/HOURS

MARKET

LOCATION

TIME OF YEAR/HOURS

MARKET

LOCATION

TIME OF YEAR/HOURS

FLEA MARKETS

MARKET

MARKET

LOCATION

LOCATION

TIME OF YEAR/HOURS

TIME OF YEAR/HOURS

MARKET

MARKET

LOCATION

LOCATION

TIME OF YEAR/HOURS

TIME OF YEAR/HOURS

MARKET

MARKET

LOCATION

LOCATION

TIME OF YEAR/HOURS

TIME OF YEAR/HOURS

CRAFT STORES

STORE

LOCATION

HOURS

PHONE NUMBER

WEBSITE

E-MAIL

STORE

LOCATION

HOURS

PHONE NUMBER

WEBSITE

E-MAIL

STORE

LOCATION

HOURS

PHONE NUMBER

WEBSITE

E-MAIL

STORE

LOCATION

HOURS

PHONE NUMBER

WEBSITE

E-MAIL

STORE

LOCATION

HOURS

PHONE NUMBER

WEBSITE

E-MAIL

STORE

LOCATION

HOURS

PHONE NUMBER

WEBSITE

E-MAIL

CRAFT STORES

STORE

LOCATION

HOURS

PHONE NUMBER

WEBSITE

E-MAIL

STORE

LOCATION

HOURS

PHONE NUMBER

WEBSITE

E-MAIL

STORE

LOCATION

HOURS

PHONE NUMBER

WEBSITE

E-MAIL

STORE

LOCATION

HOURS

PHONE NUMBER

WEBSITE

E-MAIL

STORE

LOCATION

HOURS

PHONE NUMBER

WEBSITE

E-MAIL

STORE

LOCATION

HOURS

PHONE NUMBER

WEBSITE

E-MAIL

UNUSUAL CRAFT SUPPLIES

MATERIAL

SOURCE/STORE

LOCATION/HOURS

PHONE NUMBER

WEBSITE

E-MAIL

MATERIAL

SOURCE/STORE

LOCATION/HOURS

PHONE NUMBER

WEBSITE

E-MAIL

MATERIAL

SOURCE/STORE

LOCATION/HOURS

PHONE NUMBER

WEBSITE

E-MAIL

MATERIAL

SOURCE/STORE

LOCATION/HOURS

PHONE NUMBER

WEBSITE

E-MAIL

MATERIAL

SOURCE/STORE

LOCATION/HOURS

PHONE NUMBER

WEBSITE

E-MAIL

MATERIAL

SOURCE/STORE

LOCATION/HOURS

PHONE NUMBER

WEBSITE

E-MAIL

CRAFT WEBSITES

WEBSITE

SITE OFFERING

E-MAIL

WEBSITE

SITE OFFERING

E-MAIL

WEBSITE

SITE OFFERING

E-MAIL

WEBSITE

SITE OFFERING

E-MAIL

WEBSITE

SITE OFFERING

E-MAIL

WEBSITE

SITE OFFERING

E-MAIL

WEBSITE

SITE OFFERING

E-MAIL

WEBSITE

SITE OFFERING

E-MAIL

WEBSITE

SITE OFFERING

E-MAIL

WEBSITE

SITE OFFERING

E-MAIL

CRAFT WEBSITES

WEBSITE

SITE OFFERING

E-MAIL

WEBSITE

SITE OFFERING

E-MAIL

WEBSITE

SITE OFFERING

E-MAIL

WEBSITE

SITE OFFERING

E-MAIL

WEBSITE

SITE OFFERING

E-MAIL

WEBSITE

SITE OFFERING

E-MAIL

WEBSITE

SITE OFFERING

E-MAIL

WEBSITE

SITE OFFERING

E-MAIL

WEBSITE

SITE OFFERING

E-MAIL

WEBSITE

SITE OFFERING

E-MAIL

QUILTING SUPPLIES

MATERIAL

SOURCE/STORE

LOCATION/HOURS

PHONE NUMBER

WEBSITE

E-MAIL

MATERIAL

SOURCE/STORE

LOCATION/HOURS

PHONE NUMBER

WEBSITE

E-MAIL

MATERIAL

SOURCE/STORE

LOCATION/HOURS

PHONE NUMBER

WEBSITE

E-MAIL

MATERIAL

SOURCE/STORE

LOCATION/HOURS

PHONE NUMBER

WEBSITE

E-MAIL

MATERIAL

SOURCE/STORE

LOCATION/HOURS

PHONE NUMBER

WEBSITE

E-MAIL

MATERIAL

SOURCE/STORE

LOCATION/HOURS

PHONE NUMBER

WEBSITE

E-MAIL

QUILTING SERVICES

SERVICE

CONTACT

LOCATION/HOURS

PHONE NUMBER

WEBSITE

E-MAIL

SERVICE

CONTACT

LOCATION/HOURS

PHONE NUMBER

WEBSITE

E-MAIL

SERVICE

CONTACT

LOCATION/HOURS

PHONE NUMBER

WEBSITE

E-MAIL

SERVICE

CONTACT

LOCATION/HOURS

PHONE NUMBER

WEBSITE

E-MAIL

SERVICE

CONTACT

LOCATION/HOURS

PHONE NUMBER

WEBSITE

E-MAIL

SERVICE

CONTACT

LOCATION/HOURS

PHONE NUMBER

WEBSITE

E-MAIL

QUILTING WEBSITES

WEBSITE

SITE OFFERING

E-MAIL

WEBSITE

SITE OFFERING

E-MAIL

WEBSITE

SITE OFFERING

E-MAIL

WEBSITE

SITE OFFERING

E-MAIL

WEBSITE

SITE OFFERING

E-MAIL

WEBSITE

SITE OFFERING

E-MAIL

WEBSITE

SITE OFFERING

E-MAIL

WEBSITE

SITE OFFERING

E-MAIL

WEBSITE

SITE OFFERING

E-MAIL

WEBSITE

SITE OFFERING

E-MAIL

QUILTING WEBSITES

WEBSITE

SITE OFFERING

E-MAIL

WEBSITE

SITE OFFERING

E-MAIL

WEBSITE

SITE OFFERING

E-MAIL

WEBSITE

SITE OFFERING

E-MAIL

WEBSITE

SITE OFFERING

E-MAIL

WEBSITE

SITE OFFERING

E-MAIL

WEBSITE

SITE OFFERING

E-MAIL

WEBSITE

SITE OFFERING

E-MAIL

WEBSITE

SITE OFFERING

E-MAIL

WEBSITE

SITE OFFERING

E-MAIL

SEWING COURSES

COURSE

INSTRUCTOR

LOCATION

DAY/TIME

PHONE NUMBER

WEBSITE

E-MAIL

COURSE

INSTRUCTOR

LOCATION

DAY/TIME

PHONE NUMBER

WEBSITE

E-MAIL

COURSE

INSTRUCTOR

LOCATION

DAY/TIME

PHONE NUMBER

WEBSITE

E-MAIL

COURSE

INSTRUCTOR

LOCATION

DAY/TIME

PHONE NUMBER

WEBSITE

E-MAIL

SEWING MACHINE REPAIR

STORE

LOCATION

HOURS

PHONE NUMBER

WEBSITE

E-MAIL

STORE

LOCATION

HOURS

PHONE NUMBER

WEBSITE

E-MAIL

STORE

LOCATION

HOURS

PHONE NUMBER

WEBSITE

E-MAIL

STORE

LOCATION

HOURS

PHONE NUMBER

WEBSITE

E-MAIL

STORE

LOCATION

HOURS

PHONE NUMBER

WEBSITE

E-MAIL

STORE

LOCATION

HOURS

PHONE NUMBER

WEBSITE

E-MAIL

ART/CRAFT MUSEUMS

NAME

LOCATION

HOURS

PHONE NUMBER

WEBSITE

MY FAVORITE OBJECTS ON VIEW

NAME

LOCATION

HOURS

PHONE NUMBER

WEBSITE

MY FAVORITE OBJECTS ON VIEW

NAME

LOCATION

HOURS

PHONE NUMBER

WEBSITE

MY FAVORITE OBJECTS ON VIEW

NAME

LOCATION

HOURS

PHONE NUMBER

WEBSITE

MY FAVORITE OBJECTS ON VIEW

ART/CRAFT MUSEUMS

NAME

LOCATION

HOURS

PHONE NUMBER

WEBSITE

MY FAVORITE OBJECTS ON VIEW

NAME

LOCATION

HOURS

PHONE NUMBER

WEBSITE

MY FAVORITE OBJECTS ON VIEW

NAME

LOCATION

HOURS

PHONE NUMBER

WEBSITE

MY FAVORITE OBJECTS ON VIEW

NAME

LOCATION

HOURS

PHONE NUMBER

WEBSITE

MY FAVORITE OBJECTS ON VIEW

ALSO AVAILABLE BY RODERICK KIRACOFE

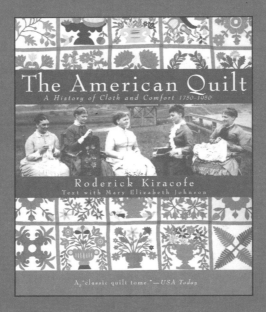

The American Quilt: A History of Cloth and Comfort 1750-1950

0-517-57535-3 hardcover, 1-4000-8096-7 paperback

The American Quilt Note Cards

0-307-23617-X